Stolen Memories

Stolen Memories

An Alzheimer's Stole Ministry and Tallit Initiative

LYNDA EVERMAN
AND
DON WENDORF

Foreword by George Vradenburg
Preface by Drexel Rayford

RESOURCE *Publications* • Eugene, Oregon

STOLEN MEMORIES
An Alzheimer's Stole Ministry and Tallit Initiative

Copyright © 2019 Lynda Everman and Don Wendorf. All rights reserved. Except for brief quotations in critical publications or reviews, no part of this book may be reproduced in any manner without prior written permission from the publisher. Write: Permissions, Wipf and Stock Publishers, 199 W. 8th Ave., Suite 3, Eugene, OR 97401.

Resource Publications
An Imprint of Wipf and Stock Publishers
199 W. 8th Ave., Suite 3
Eugene, OR 97401

www.wipfandstock.com

PAPERBACK ISBN: 978-1-5326-8333-6
HARDCOVER ISBN: 978-1-5326-8334-3
EBOOK ISBN: 978-1-5326-8335-0

Manufactured in the U.S.A.   JULY 1, 2019

Dedication

"Then I heard the voice of the Lord saying,
'Whom shall I send? And who will go for us?'
And I said, 'Here am I. Send me!'"

—Isaiah 6:8 (NIV)

Pastor, pioneer in the field of spirituality and aging, mentor, author, activist, chaplain, champion, and humble Christian—these words barely begin to describe Rev. Dr. Richard L. Morgan. And, so it is, in celebration of and gratitude for our dear friend and in recognition of his lifetime of service on behalf of those with Alzheimer's and related dementias and their care partners, families and friends, that we dedicate this book.

Contents

Mission Statement / ix
Foreword by George Vradenburg / xi
Preface by Drexel Rayford / xv
Acknowledgments / xix

1. Dementia: Stolen Memories and More / 1
2. How the Alzheimer's Stole Ministry and Tallit Initiative Began / 5
3. The Pastor's Stole and Its Significance / 10
4. My First Stoles / 12
5. Clergy Advocates / 18
6. Instructions / 65
   A. What You'll Need To Get Started / 65
   B. How to Make a Basic Stole / 67
   C. Stepping Up to a Contoured Neckline / 72
   D. How to Make a Stole Style Tallit / 79
7. Conclusion / 82

About the Authors / 83
In Memoriam / 86
Bibliography / 87

Mission Statement

WHAT BEGAN AS AN Alzheimer's Stole Ministry quickly became the Alzheimer's Stole Ministry and Tallit Initiative which is much like the stoles and tallitot themselves: a diverse patchwork of individuals joined together by common threads of caring and the wish to use our time and talents to support and advocate with and for those impacted by dementia. And to do this in a way that adds a bit of beauty and joy to the journey. We see the Alzheimer's stoles and tallitot as vital and visual symbols of our efforts to initiate or expand dementia friendly faith communities.

Foreword

HOW GENEROUS IS LYNDA Everman? When the story of an Alzheimer's treatment or cure is told, Lynda will be a central and beautiful part of that story. She lost her husband, Richard, to Alzheimer's and her father to vascular dementia. Since then she has been a force in the fight to stop Alzheimer's and a passionate advocate for those living with the disease and their families. Lynda has given countless hours to support UsAgainstAlzheimer's. She successfully advocated for an Alzheimer's semipostal stamp and leads a Dementia Friendly Faith Initiative in Alabama. She spearheaded publication of three interfaith books to support caregivers and worship for those living with dementia. Lynda was inspired to begin this stole ministry and tallit initiative in gratitude for her partnership with the people you'll meet in these pages.

When I heard that Lynda had offered to create a tallit for me, I could only respond, "How generous is Lynda Everman?" As you will see, her generosity is without any discernible limit. Her pastors' stoles and tallitot honor those living with Alzheimer's and provoke conversation and understanding. The stoles and prayer shawls represented here are beautiful, creative symbols of Tikkun Olam—the healing of the world, including the prevention and cure of Alzheimer's. These stoles and prayer shawls will, I hope, inspire you to action—to learn about Alzheimer's, support those in your community facing this often deeply isolating disease, and become educated about the importance of valuing brain health and the need for more Alzheimer's research funding. My "Everman tallit" offers a connection to my daily work, to my beloved late wife, Trish, and to the millions of people we serve. Lynda chose fabrics that are symbols of my Jewish faith, including the Hebrew alphabet, menorah, Star of David and peace doves. Trish and I watched her mother, Bea Lerner, succumb to Alzheimer's. Bea was a wonderful woman—fearless and brilliant. Politics was her passion. She was a Democratic leader in New Jersey and credited with winning the state for President John F. Kennedy because of her mobilization of a massive demonstration on the weekend before the 1960 election. As Trish often said, her mother was larger than life with unmatched humor and style, including her signature pearls, which are represented in my tallit.

The forget-me-not flowers are a reminder of Trish, the love of my life and funniest woman I have ever known. Trish understood that the world needed to be healed and transformed, and she lived this in her fierce commitment to finding an Alzheimer's cure. She and I started UsAgainstAlzheimer's to honor her mother and ensure that our children and grandchildren—and your children and grandchildren—don't have to fear this disease.

FOREWORD

5.8 million Americans are living with Alzheimer's and more than 16 million people are family or unpaid caregivers. UsAgainstAlzheimer's is on a mission to expand the means of prevention and treatment by disrupting the business-as-usual status quo. We are mobilizing stakeholders across the Alzheimer's landscape, creating an environment of collaboration and innovation while supporting the often-unheard voices of those disparately affected patients and caregivers, particularly within communities of color, women and veterans. Faith leaders and people of faith are setting a powerful example by welcoming these individuals and families into their communities and ensuring that they are treated with love, dignity and compassion.

While Lynda designed and created the stoles and prayer shawls shown here, I hope you will be inspired to join her. Together we're going to beat Alzheimer's. And I will treasure my tallit as a tangible reminder of the many reasons that inspire me and give me hope.

GEORGE VRADENBURG
Chairman and Co-Founder, UsAgainstAlzheimer's

Preface

LYNDA EVERMAN HAS MADE some astonishingly beautiful clergy stoles and tallitot, so I was honored when she and her husband, Don Wendorf, asked me to write this Preface. We share a vested interest in addressing the kind of isolation and loneliness that compound the pain of those suffering from cognitive impairment, along with those who care for them. Currently, I work with the University of Alabama at Birmingham (UAB) Medicine's Department of Pastoral Care. We're building a hospital-based community partnership aimed at nurturing healing communities of support for the families of discharged patients who might otherwise fade from view due to the unique pressures of caring daily for a person with progressive incapacities.

There is some irony in my writing about clergy vestments since I'm a Baptist clergyman. For the most part, Baptist clergy don't wear special ministerial garb. I grew up in First Baptist Church, Charlotte, North Carolina and I never saw my pastor wear a robe, let alone a stole. He always wore a suit. Of course, they were tailor-made suits and cost a whole lot more than the polyester specials my dad bought at Sears, but even so, from a distance he just looked like a branch bank manager when he stood in the pulpit.

Then, I went to college. After college, I lived in Austria. After Austria, I came back to the States, attended seminary, earned a PhD in the psychology of religion, worked on a psychiatric ward, and piled up mileage as a senior pastor in three different churches. Most recently, I've worked in the Department of Pastoral Care at

Preface

UAB. You might say, "Aha! I know where he's going with this. He saw the world, got educated, and left the Baptist tradition."

Nope. I'm still a Baptist, but my experience of moving from a childhood religion to an adult faith, of encountering a tidal wave of human suffering both in clinical settings and in the congregations I served, has led me to the desire that whenever I lead in worship, I offer something more than a physical image calling to mind a business executive. The clergy who lead the Baptist church of which I am a member wear robes and stoles, as I have now for the better half of my pastoral career. The colors and symbols draped across the bodies of pastoral servants can remind us of unseen realities infusing our universe—if we have eyes to see.

And that brings me back to the stoles and tallitot Lynda has made. When clergy persons choose to wear one of these, one of the most tragic of those unseen realities meets the eye. Multiple professionals in our society have sounded the alarm that we have a growing epidemic of loneliness, with Alzheimer's and related dementias being particularly isolating spiritually, mentally and physically. I don't have space here to detail what research and experience make evident about the depth of the problem. The facts are indisputable, however, and as one researcher has said, unless action is taken the epidemic will engulf us by the year 2030. When someone sees a clergy person wearing one of these stoles or tallitot, the reality of that problem becomes visible.

They remind us that isolation, loneliness, and lack of belonging actually have a profound negative impact on a human being's cellular make-up. The research I mentioned has proven this beyond doubt. Loneliness actually reduces immunity and increases inflammation, which together weave a biochemical environment ripe for the growth of all manner of disease, including many forms of cancer, cardio-vascular distress, and—especially relevant to this book—cognitive decline. The Alzheimer's Stole Ministry and Tallit Initiative stands for physical and spiritual well being, not just of the Alzheimer's or dementia patients, but for their caregivers, as well.

Preface

These stoles and tallitot also remind us that those with dementia or Alzheimer's aren't the only ones who suffer the effects of loneliness. Caregivers, too, experience isolation as the crowd of family and friends thins over time. Some caregivers feel as if it's their responsibility alone to tend to the needs of their affected loved one and they have a difficult time letting others in. Sometimes, others don't know how to support the caregiver. More often, as persons dealing with cognitive decline interact less with folks beyond the home, the house becomes an island with no bridge.

So, these stoles and tallitot remind us that we are called to build bridges. In fact, just as the data show that isolation increases the incidence of disease, the consistent presence of a supporting community reduces the incidence of disease. Research shows that with healthy interaction with other human beings, cognitive decline may be slowed, perhaps halted, and in some cases, possibly even reversed. When we consistently reach out, we see to it that those who care for persons living with dementia and Alzheimer's experience intimacy, understanding, and—in a word—Love.

The Alzheimer's Stole Ministry and Tallit Initiative proclaims that *community is medicine*.

So, if you're clergy, get yourself one of these vestments. If you're not clergy, make one as a gift for your own pastor, priest, or rabbi. They can serve to challenge us to build bridges to those otherwise trapped on islands of isolation, to look for and see those who've become invisible. They'll also celebrate that when we build and cross those bridges, we heal disease by our simple presence. Wearing these will elegantly remind us of the medicine in the community we weave together.

Indeed, for Alzheimer's and dementia sufferers, as well as for their caregivers, *community is medicine*.

Rev. Dr. Drexel Rayford
Dept. of Pastoral Care, UAB Medicine

Acknowledgments

WE WANT TO THANK Ginny Biggar, Director of Communities for UsAgainstAlzheimer's, for her constant support and encouragement, as well as her expert help and wise counsel, in the preparation of this book and in all our dementia friendly faith communities efforts.

1

Dementia
Stolen Memories and More

"... Surely the Lord is in this place, and I was not aware of it."
—Genesis 28:16 (NIV)

DEMENTIA IS A GENERAL term for loss of memory and other cognitive abilities severe enough to interfere with daily life. Alzheimer's is the most common type of dementia, but there are many kinds. Some of the ones you've most likely heard about are Frontotemporal dementia, Lewy Body dementia, Vascular dementia, Parkinson's disease dementia, and Mixed dementia. All are neurological disorders resulting in a progressive and irreversible loss of brain functioning affecting memory, thinking, and behavior; and, eventually causing death.

While we most commonly think in terms of being deeply forgetful, symptoms of dementia may include difficulties with communication and language; ability to focus, pay attention and retain information; gait and balance; and visual and spatial perception. Other symptoms may include faulty judgment, difficult or inappropriate behaviors, restlessness or agitation, and lack of personal hygiene. In the later stages, a person with dementia will most likely be unable to recognize family, friends, and once familiar objects and places; may lose the ability to swallow; and may experience incontinence.

It's not our intention to focus on one type of dementia while neglecting others, but to use the word "Alzheimer's" inclusively as it is intended and used in the National Alzheimer's Project Act (NAPA) signed into law by President Obama in January 2011, to mean "Alzheimer's and related dementias." This law calls for an aggressive and coordinated national plan to accelerate research on Alzheimer's disease and related dementias, and to provide better clinical care and services for people living with dementia and their families. So when you see ads on TV or posts on social media about Alzheimer's awareness, please know that this is simply a "shorthand" referring to all forms of dementia.

According to the Alzheimer's Association's 2019 Alzheimer's Disease Facts and Figures Report (available online at www.alz.org/alzheimers-dementia/facts-figures), there are 5.8 million Americans living with Alzheimer's and they are being cared for by 16.1 million family caregivers who, in 2019, will provide an estimated 18.5 billion hours of difficult, selfless, and unpaid care with a financial value of more than $234 billion. With a new diagnosis every 65 seconds, Alzheimer's has the unhappy distinction of being the sixth leading cause of death in the United States, killing more of our loved ones than breast cancer and prostrate cancer combined. The National Institute on Aging suggests that the disorder may rank third, just behind heart disease and cancer, as a cause of death for older people as underreporting of Alzheimer's on death certificates is a well-known phenomenon. Whether third or sixth, it is undisputedly the only top 10 deadly disease not to have an effective means of prevention, treatment or cure.

While the human and financial costs are staggering (How does one even begin to comprehend 18.5 billion hours of caregiving and financial costs of $234 billion?), the simple truth is this: one person diagnosed with dementia is one too many! I (for the rest of the book the personal pronouns "I" and "me" refer to Lynda) know this firsthand as I was the sole caregiver for 18 long and onerous years (1994–2012) for my Dad and my late husband, Richard. Alzheimer's took both of them—took them twice—too soon and too unkindly, and, in its wake, left me with a fierce determination that no other family should have to endure the loss, the pain, and the loneliness of this most merciless disease. All of us affected by Alzheimer's feel an urgency to stop this disease.

It was this experience and the bold vision of UsAgainstAlzheimer's (UsA2) co-founders George and Trish Vradenburg to find a cure by 2020 that first drew me to their organization where I became involved as a founding member of two of UsA2's national networks: ActivistsAgainstAlzheimer's and WomenAgainstAlzheimer's. At any given moment we, as individuals, have two options: we can choose to give in to the enormity of our grief or we can choose to go forward with hope. In UsAgainstAlzheimer's, I found a community of activists who chose hope and who, with urgency, passion and perseverance, chose to engage in advocacy that would change the trajectory of this disease. This includes such things as vigorous lobbying for increased federal Alzheimer's research funding through the National Institutes of Health, promoting legislation to address barriers to care, addressing disparities in communities of color, tackling the heavy and disproportionate burden of Alzheimer's on women and promoting women's—and therefore, families'—brain health, engaging our nation's most respected researchers to analyze and report on the drug pipe line, and more.

It was also during this time that fellow advocate, Kathy Siggins, and I enlisted the support of UsAgainstAlzheimer's, Alzheimer's Association, Alzheimer's Foundation of America and other major Alzheimer's advocacy organizations in conducting a national campaign resulting in the issuance of the first ever Alzheimer's Disease Research Semipostal Stamp. Semipostal stamps, of which there are only three, are first-class mail postage stamps that are issued and sold at a price above the first-class mail rate to raise funds for designated causes, in this case, research for Alzheimer's and related dementias. In its first fifteen months on the market, the Alzheimer's stamp raised over $840,000 for Alzheimer's research funded through the National Institutes of Health. The postage stamps are available at most post offices, online at usps.com, and by toll-free phone order at 1-800 STAMP-24. (https://about.usps.com/corporate-social-responsibility/semipostals.htm)

As engaged as I was in advocacy, I still felt something was missing. I kept thinking of the advancements that had been made in other areas of health and social justice when men and women of faith became involved. I came to believe that a network of multi-faith clergy, laity, and faith organizations would offer an important and powerful perspective in our collective efforts to fight this disease. In 2014 with the support of UsAgainstAlzheimer's and a small group of volunteers including Rev. Dr. Richard L. Morgan, Rabbi Steven M. Glazer, noted neurologist and author Dr. Daniel C. Potts, and Boston University senior and neuroscience major Max Wallack, we recruited over 100 founding members and convened ClergyAgainstAlzheimer's, calling for urgent action to stop this disease and for better, more compassionate care for those with Alzheimer's and their families.

Our members believe that living with value and purpose is a basic human right, and to that end, we are working to create dementia friendly faith communities that are welcoming to all despite the limitations of cognitive impairment—communities that enable worship, support care partners, educate about dementia, and promote brain health.

All proceeds from the sale of this book support the work of ClergyAgainstAlzheimer's: www.clergyagainstalzheimers.org.

2

How the Alzheimer's Stole Ministry and Tallit Initiative Began

"Therefore, as God's chosen people, holy and dearly loved, clothe yourselves with compassion, kindness, humility, gentleness and patience."
–Colossians 3:12 (NIV)

2018 WAS A BUSY year for our Alzheimer's advocacy. In addition to promoting sales of the newly released Alzheimer's Disease Research Semipostal Stamp, my husband, Dr. Don Wendorf, and I served as Senior Editors for the anthology, *Dementia-friendly Worship: A Multifaith Handbook for Chaplains, Clergy and Faith Communities*.

ClergyAgainstAlzheimer's in collaboration with Cognitive Dynamics Foundation and Dementia Friendly Alabama also received a grant that allowed us to visit faith leaders and congregational care staff in the greater Birmingham, Alabama area to provide them with resources to encourage and expand their work as dementia friendly—actually, dementia active—faith communities.

In the course of this work, an already familiar theme was again highly evident: the powerful capacity of the expressive arts—music, painting, photography, poetry, dance, fabric and textile arts, etc.—for emotional nurturing, communication, connection, building relationships and healing. Sharing feelings and experiences in these largely nonverbal ways often allows people to transform and transcend their deepest worries and concerns. I have experienced this many times over the years in my personal involvement with textile arts and was captivated by the use of therapies employing art, music, and story telling in an innovative, intergenerational adult day care program, Bringing Art to Life, at Caring Days in Tuscaloosa, developed by our Cognitive Dynamics partner, Dr. Daniel Potts. Danny's father, Lester Potts, had learned to paint water colors after being diagnosed with Alzheimer's and it was instrumental in giving him greater quality of life and self-esteem. It also allowed for a renewal of the close relationships of Lester with his family. I now provide personalized lap size quilts for each participant living with dementia in that program. I literally "quilt their stories" as a means of preserving and honoring their life histories. As a former caregiver, it's a way for me to offer comfort and support to those now facing dementia.

Don, a musician himself, had experienced the healing power of music in caring for his late wife Susan—and in caring for himself—as he wrote his book, *Caregiver Carols: a Musical, Emotional Memoir,* to help other caregivers with their emotional struggles. He wrote his book largely in a song lyric/rhyming verse format. He wrote and recorded two selections for Susan and it was one of these that led to our meeting, when he submitted it for ClergyAgainstAlzheimer's first book, *Seasons of Caring: Meditations for Alzheimer's and Dementia Caregivers.* Don regularly plays music now for a session of Bringing Art to Life, as well as in assisted living and memory care units, and is constantly feeling the tremendous impact of the expressive arts on the mental, emotional and spiritual health of all concerned, including himself.

This theme of using expressive arts emerged repeatedly in our handbook on dementia worship as almost all of our contributors recommended using them, especially music, in designing worship experiences for persons living with dementia, as well as their caregivers and families and congregations. They told of how the old familiar hymns, in particular, helped people enter into the sacred space of worship and actively participate in it as members of their faith community, sometimes even if they were almost mute the rest of the time. People who could not otherwise communicate or remember much about their current situation, could sing all the words of the hymns of their childhood. Similar things happened with pictures, painting, and photographs as when our friend, Dr. Richard Morgan, showed memory care residents copies of Lester Potts' paintings. These images sparked many memories and the sharing of stories, that resulted in another book, *Treasure for Alzheimer's: Reflecting on experiences with the art of Lester E. Potts, Jr.,* co-authored by Richard and Danny.

Coincidentally, as we sat in pastors' offices during our visits, we became aware of another form of visual, fabric art—actually, liturgical art—the pastors' stoles—some hanging on the backs of doors and some beautifully displayed. As we commented on the stoles, we began to hear deeply personal stories of people and events that were meaningful to the clergy members. More and more, we were struck by the juxtaposition of the pastors' stoles "holding memories" and of dementia stealing memories. As a quilter and someone who has always loved the textile arts, the idea of fabric and stoles holding memories and telling stories resonated strongly with me. I began to think about what a pastor's stole could convey in terms of support and advocacy with Alzheimer's and related dementias.

Obviously, the pastor, priest, or rabbi is at the center of each faith community and wearing the Alzheimer's stole or tallit is meant to increase awareness, to share stories, and to spark dialogue and ideas. It may start the exchange of educational information about dementia issues or caregiving tips or advice. It may allow the expression of individual concerns or the tremendous emotional struggles someone is experiencing, either as a caregiver or as a person trying to live as well as possible with the challenges of this disease. It may allow members of the congregation to talk openly about previously taboo topics—guilt, grief, anger, fear and frustration to name a few—and help decrease some of the stigma around dementia. It may lead to prayers and blessings on behalf of everyone involved and bring the perspective of faith and a caring community into the arena.

Even more, wearing the Alzheimer's stole or tallit is meant to inspire and energize: to generate real and concrete action to make a difference in the lives of all affected by these diseases. Insight and knowledge need to be translated into specific, practical, helpful actions. Early on, ClergyAgainstAlzheimer's adopted this simple, yet powerful African proverb as our motto: "When you pray, move your feet." This might mean that congregations begin to change the physical layout of their church to be more safe and navigable for persons challenged by impaired perceptions, memory or judgment. Worship services may be made more dementia friendly by being shorter or by including more familiar hymns or by using more artistic and visual cues to help people enter into a sacred space.

Congregations may want to provide a library of resources about dementia or invite speakers to their Sunday school classes or senior groups to address topics related to dementia, caregiving, brain health or the spirituality of aging. Others may begin their own initiative with new or existing sewing/quilting groups making personalized stoles and tallitot for clergy. Lay ministries could arrange to visit people affected by dementia in their homes or in senior care facilities. As Dr. Richard Morgan reminds us, "The ability to provide needed information is valuable, but the essence of spiritual care comes from the very fact of the visit and the willingness of the visitor to take the time to listen." Those with dementia and their caregivers are frequently isolated and have few, if any, opportunities to share their concerns and their grief with others. Richard teaches that, "Whoever visits brings the presence of God to the caregiver and receiver. The visitor is Christ's heart, ears, eyes, and hands." He encourages us to "Visit regularly and often!"

Youth or other groups could give very practical assistance such as doing yard work or shopping or home repairs or providing companionship experiences. Churches and synagogues may even decide to create respite care programs for care partners to bring their loved ones with dementia so that everyone can get a break or enjoy the fellowship of others in "memory cafés" or special events. Faith communities may begin expressive arts (music, visual art, dance, etc.) programs or become collection sites for gently used devices to make individualized music play lists as with social worker Dan Cohen's Music and Memory program (www.musicandmemory.org). Some congregations may want to open up day care programs on a full or part-time basis.

These are just a few of the kinds of responses congregations may make to persons living with dementia, their care partners and their loved ones. For more ideas, please visit our website: www.clergyagainstalzheimers.org. The document, "Creating Dementia Friendly Faith Communities," provides steps to help you get started. The purpose of the Alzheimer's Stole Ministry and Tallit Initiative is to create or expand dementia friendly faith communities—communities in which these and other ideas can be put into motion. Motion. Action. "When you pray, move your feet." Or your hands and fingers!

3

The Pastor's Stole and Its Significance

According to Wikipedia, a stole is a Christian liturgical garment, varying in length from about 7-1/2 to 9 feet, that is worn around the back of the neck and allowed to hang in parallel bands down the front. It may then be tied or untied, depending on the particular denomination. It typically is decorated with Christian symbols and often has fringe at the bottom. Its history may go back into Old Testament times to the fringed garment Jews wore as a remembrance of God's commandments (Numbers 15:37-41).

There are many theories as to the origin of the stole. It may be derived from the Jewish prayer mantle, shawl or tallit or it may be from a kind of liturgical napkin (orarium) which could symbolize the towel Christ used to dry the feet of His disciples after washing them. Or stoles may be a symbol of the bonds that tied up Christ in His passion—the yoke of Christ—or the yoke of sacrifice and service. Others relate the stole to the Roman Empire where it was a scarf of office among Imperial officials to designate rank.

Today the stole indicates that someone has been ordained or consecrated as a member of the clergy. In some denominations deacons also wear stoles, although often just over the left shoulder and fastened together in the middle under the right arm. Chaplains

The Pastor's Stole and Its Significance

sometimes wear shorter "visitation" stoles that are more practical for their place of ministry such as hospital settings. The color and design of stoles may signify a particular time in the liturgical calendar. They all vary considerably in length, width, design, fabric, decorations, symbols, fringe or no fringe, etc. and there does not seem to be a "one size fits all" standard.

Stoles also carry individual histories and have a wide range of personal and emotional significance attached to them. For example, they are often given as gifts upon ordination or some other special occasion. Many are handed down from one clergy member to a member of the next generation. They may be given to mark the beginning of a ministry or in remembrance of a special event, such as a trip to the Holy Land. In our visits to local churches, we saw breast cancer stoles, youth minister stoles adorned with children's handprints, white wedding stoles, and one passed on by a pastor's widow to the current pastor. Some stoles are worn to honor or pray for or remember a loved one. Stoles are multifaceted and capable of holding and expressing many deep and meaningful feelings, ideas, and memories. It's all of these things—their beauty, symbolism and histories—that attract me and cause me to appreciate how impactful they are for clergy ministering to and advocating for persons with dementia and their loved ones. I began to see the stoles as a ministry in themselves.

As you will see later on, I began making Christian stoles for an Alzheimer's "ministry" as that was what I knew about and was encountering in our dementia friendly faith community visits. However, we were thrilled to find out, first from our friend and network co-founder Rabbi Steve Glazer (see below), that many Jews wear a stole-like style of the traditional prayer shawl or "tallit" and the whole project then expanded to become the Alzheimer's Stole Ministry and Tallit Initiative, which is very much in keeping with the multifaith basis of our networks and writings. Later still we also visited a pastor of a Unitarian Universalist church who requested a stole and learned that she doesn't identify herself as only Christian or Jewish and I had to adjust my use of religious symbols in her stole accordingly.

4

My First Stoles

Rev. Dr. Cynthia Huling Hummel is an Alzheimer's advocate, an author, an artist, a musician, and a Presbyterian (USA) pastor living with dementia. She is also a courageous woman, eager to destigmatize Alzheimer's. I first learned about Cynthia when I read an online article (www.womansday.com/health-fitness/05754/im-living-with-early-alzheimers-disease/) she had written for Woman's Day magazine in 2017 that ended with this paragraph:

> Life doesn't end after an Alzheimer's diagnosis. Everyone faces crises, but the real challenge is moving from "why me?" to "what next?" I know things will slow down in the future. But I don't dwell on the future. I tell people to focus on each and every day and the blessings in that day, and I can't just stand in the pulpit and preach it, I've got to live it.

I knew right then that I wanted to meet Cynthia, so when we began working on our book on dementia worship, we reached out to ask her if she would contribute a chapter. She generously agreed and gave us not just one chapter, but four, and we immediately became friends and advocacy partners.

Cynthia introduced us to her newest book, *UnMasking Alzheimer's: The Memories Behind the Masks*, in which she shares photographs of thirty masks she created along with her reflections on the challenges and hopes of living well with an Alzheimer's diagnosis. Her book gives a very realistic insight into what it's like to have dementia, without being hopeless or terrifying. Her story is heartrending, but also filled with faith, joy, friendship, and purpose. It is a book I wish I had had during my years as a caregiver because it is only the person living with dementia who can tell you what it means to live with that diagnosis. In *Unmasking Alzheimer's,* she illuminates the transformative power of the arts and encourages readers to look beyond the masks of cognitive impairment to reach and connect with the person who is still very much present. Cynthia is a sterling example of what people living with dementia can still do and are doing!

I also asked Cynthia to write a prayer to share with members of our network during World Alzheimer's Month. This is the international campaign every September to raise awareness that every three seconds someone in the world develops dementia, to support those affected, and to challenge the stigma that surrounds dementia.

I surprised Cynthia with the first stole I made, to convey our deep appreciation for her friendship and ministry and in honor of World Alzheimer's Month. Also, to let her know that when things got tough, as they surely will, we will be here with our love, our prayers, and our support.

One of the main design elements in Cynthia's stole (and all subsequent stoles) is the inclusion of the purple ribbon as it is widely recognized as a symbol for Alzheimer's awareness.

Rev. Dr. Cynthia Huling Hummel, Presbyterian (USA), Elmira, NY

A Prayer for World Alzheimer's Month
By Rev. Dr. Cynthia Huling Hummel

Dear Lord,

    Bless those of us who are living with a diagnosis of Alzheimer's or a related dementia. When days are difficult, wrap us in a blanket of your love and comfort us with your presence and your peace. When nights are dark, give us a star to follow—a nightlight in the heavens to remind us that you are there—guarding and guiding us and lighting our paths. When we are discouraged, give us hope. When we are hopeless, give us faith. When we are weary, carry us close to your heart. When we feel depressed or angry, soothe us. Wipe away our tears and our fears and help us to move from "Why Me?" to "What Next?"

We thank you for our care partners, for our family and friends who are walking with us on this strange and difficult journey. Give us all strength and courage and a sense of purpose as we join our hands and hearts to help others we meet along the way.

Help us all to cultivate an attitude of gratitude each and every day. Remind us to look for blessings in everyday, and holy moments: walking in the rain, singing a familiar song, reminiscing over old photos.

Lord, we pray for the doctors and nurses and all who care about us and for us. We pray for the researchers who are searching for treatments, therapies and cures. Most of all, Lord, we pray for a world without Alzheimer's.

Thank you! Amen.

I'd been thinking about making a stole for our dear friend and fellow ClergyAgainstAlzheimer's founder, Rev. Dr. Richard L. Morgan, for some time. This idea came from his comment in a book that he co-wrote with Dr. Jane Marie Thibault in 2009, *No Act of Love Is Ever Wasted: The Spirituality of Caring for Persons with Dementia,* about using memory cues and visual and tactile symbols—such as the sign of the cross, the use of uplifted hands in blessing, passing the peace or wearing a stole—to trigger memories. He commented, "It's amazing how persistent the memory for things said, done or worn in churches over a lifetime can be."

At age 90 and with neuropathy and other health issues and concerns, including caring for his wife, Alice Ann, with her cognitive impairment, Richard still continues to minister to those with memory disorders. I wanted to thank him for his lifetime of serving others and hoped that as he slipped the stole around his shoulders he would feel our love and gratitude.

Since his stole was also meant to provide visual cues to those he visited in memory care, I carefully chose fabrics with well known Christian symbols: the words "Love" and "Joy" with a scriptural reference ["This is love: not that we loved God, but that He loved us and sent His Son as an atoning sacrifice for our sins." –John 4:10 (NIV);"Rejoice in the Lord Always."–Philippians 4:4 (NIV)], fish and cross icons, old fashioned churches, and the peace dove with an olive branch signifying the Holy Spirit.

When Cynthia learned that I was making stoles for other pastors and clergy members, she wrote this special blessing that I now include with each gift:

> A Special Blessing for An Alzheimer's Stole
> and for the One Who Wears It
> By Rev. Dr. Cynthia Huling Hummel
> (A Presbyterian [USA] Pastor who is living with Alzheimer's)
>
> God of Blessings, We ask that you bless this stole and bless the one who wears it as s/he answers your call to serve your beloved people: those with Alzheimer's and related dementias and their care partners, families and friends. Thank you for calling (Insert Clergy Member's Name Here) to this special ministry of remembrance! Remind us all of who we are and whose we are: God's beloved!
>
> God of the Journey, We walk together, hand-in-hand and heart-to-heart. We walk with a purpose: to support and care for one another on this difficult and uncertain journey. Help us to remember that you will never leave us or forsake us, but that you walk beside us in times of pain, sorrow and joy. Tears may linger through the night, but through your grace, joy will come in the morning. Give us all strength and courage for the journey ahead.
>
> Creator God, Just as this Alzheimer's stole was created from many pieces of colorful cloth, stitch us together into a new creation: united in purpose and passion and in our shared dream for a world without Alzheimer's. We join hearts and voices in prayer for advocates who speak on our behalf—for us and with us—and for researchers who are diligently seeking a cure, working on treatments, and developing interventions. We thank you for their devotion to these tasks.
>
> Remembering One, We know that you will never forget us for YOU have written our names on the palm

MY FIRST STOLES

of your hand and hold us ever so close to your heart. So please dear Lord, bless this stole and bless the one who wears it. Amen!

Made especially for you with deep appreciation by Lynda Everman, Founding Member, ClergyAgainstAlzheimer's

5

Clergy Advocates
Photos and Reflections

"The Lord is close to the brokenhearted
and saves those who are crushed in spirit."

−Psalm 34:18 (NIV)

Cynthia was thrilled with her stole, which led quickly to a flurry of Facebook posts ("Love my new pastor's stole handmade by my dear friend Lynda Everman to commemorate World Alzheimer's Month. Her beautiful gift makes my heart sing!") of photos of her wearing it at numerous events on behalf of the Alzheimer's Association where she was a presenter, as well as from the pulpit of First Presbyterian Church of Pulteney in Pulteney, NY. She labeled her pastor's stole "liturgical art" and saw it as a loving symbol of our friendship and shared ministry.

Later, when asked to share her personal reactions or emotions about the stole and what it and the Stole Ministry represents to her, she shared this poignant reflection:

The Gift of a Stole: An Affirmation of My Ministry

> "Be strong and courageous. Do not be afraid or terrified because of them, for the Lord your God goes with you; he will never leave you nor forsake you."
> –Deuteronomy 31:6 (NIV)

When I received the beautiful hand-crafted stole from Lynda Everman, I cried. It was such a wonderful surprise—such a gift of love, and such an affirmation of my call—a call that I, quite honestly, was slow to embrace.

When I took it out of the mailing envelope and put the colorful stole around my shoulders, I could feel its power! I imagined God smiling and whispering in my ear: "Cynthia, it's true. Alzheimer's is your ministry! This is what I prepared you for. Wear this stole and remember the work I have called you to do." Wow.

Truthfully, it took me awhile to get to this place of acceptance. I did NOT want Alzheimer's and I certainly didn't want an Alzheimer's ministry. For a long time, I was pretty angry at God. I mean, it just seemed so unfair that after years and years of study and preparation for ministry, that I was no longer able to as serve as a Pastor because of my cognitive problems. But I couldn't do it anymore. I couldn't remember my people and what they had shared with me. I felt defeated, broken, lonely and useless.

Thankfully, I remembered my mother's words: "No one ever promised you a rose garden." and "Into every life, a little rain must fall." Our mom, Claire Matthews Huling, wanted us, her children, to understand at an early age that no one was exempt from pain and sorrow and that everyone would encounter difficult times. Mom taught us that in times of trouble we were to "Pick ourselves up, brush ourselves off and start all over again." Mom had a deep and abiding faith and her remedy for hard times was straight forward: prayer and helping others. These two practices have shaped my life in profound ways and I have learned two simple truths:

when we help others, we help ourselves; and prayer changes us as we grow closer to God.

I've spent a lot of time walking and talking with God and with others who like myself, are on this strange and often frightening Alzheimer's journey—and with the "care-ers", who walk beside us in love. An Alzheimer's ministry isn't one sided. It goes both ways and I will tell you this: I've received far more than I have given. I know now, that THIS is the ministry that God prepared me for. The reality is that God loves to use broken people to walk with others who are broken and in doing so, we become wounded healers to each other. By sharing our struggles, our pain, our tears and our fears, we become vulnerable and it's in this heart-shaped place, that healing begins to happen.

When people ask how I'm feeling, my answer is immediate and simple: I feel blessed. I thank God for this amazing ministry, a ministry I would have never chosen but seems to have chosen me. I also thank God for my wonderful mother Claire who, like me, had Alzheimer's. She went home to our Lord in 2014 and there is not a day that goes by, when I don't think of her and when I do, I thank her for her wisdom, her faith and most of all, her love!

Rev. Dr. Cynthia Huling Hummel, Presbyterian (USA), Elmira, NY

Richard Morgan, too, was deeply moved by my gift and wrote these kind words: "A British poet, Alfred Terhune, wrote, 'In love and divinity, what's most worth saying can't be put into words.' I am overwhelmed by the beautiful, colorful stole you made for me. It was surely a work of dedication and love. Tomorrow I will be visiting Memory Care and I shall wear it to show the residents. I am sure they will have a great time identifying with the words and symbols on the stole. Although I no longer lead worship, I can wear it in my visitation of people with dementia. Again, I am indebted to you and Don for your constant friendship and support. The stole symbolizes that friendship and will be cherished as long as I live."

Later, he went on to say, "Your stole has much use. I use it in my visits to Memory Care. Since I do not lead worship anymore,

I loaned it to (Chaplain) Dave Fetterman who wears it when he leads worship in Memory Care AND at chapel; I will show it to my support group this month." I love it: a *shared* ministry and a *shared* stole!

Then a few months later Richard told us that he had added this codicil to his will: "That the Alzheimer's stole created for me by Lynda Everman be placed on the altar next to the Urn containing my cremains at my Memorial Service. A witness to my ministry for people with Alzheimer's." I didn't expect a reaction like this to my stole; I was amazed at the impact of this little piece of liturgical art.

Rev. Dr. Richard L. Morgan, Presbyterian (USA), North Huntingdon, PA

I was very moved by Cynthia's and Richard's responses and so I kept making and gifting more stoles, thinking how wonderful it would be for pastors to wear Alzheimer's stoles especially in those months where brain health and Alzheimer's are nationally recognized and there are campaigns to raise awareness and end the stigma of mental and cognitive dysfunction that comes in large part, from silence: June (Brain Health), September (World Alzheimer's Month), and November (National Alzheimer's Awareness and National Caregivers Month). If we had pastors don their stoles, speak from the pulpit, pray and encourage their congregations to help as they saw fit, what a significant movement this would be!

In September 2018 Don and I attended UsAgainstAlzheimer's annual summit in DC and yet another use and opportunity for the Alzheimer's stole presented itself when one of our attendees, Rev. Jason Carson Wilson, a United Church of Christ minister, came to the conference and made his visits to members of Congress wearing a clergy stole. His presence with his stole was a most powerful message of faith based advocacy!

Rev. Kathy Fogg Berry, Interdenominational Christian, Richmond, VA
Rev. Cynthia Abrams, United Methodist, Manassas, VA
Rev. Jason Carson Wilson, United Church of Christ, Washington, DC

As I mentioned above, the stoles include fabric with purple ribbons. I hope that the purple ribbon and all it stands for will become as ubiquitous as the pink ribbon is for Breast Cancer awareness. In fact, since the back of each Alzheimer's stole is made with purple fabric, each is actually a purple Alzheimer's awareness "ribbon!"

Backs of stoles folded in shape of Alzheimer's awareness ribbons

Rev. Dr. Dedric A. Cowser is the Senior Pastor of New Beginnings United Methodist Church, a predominantly African American congregation, in Birmingham, Alabama. As part of our dementia friendly outreach, we wrote to Dr. Cowser asking if he might be interested in meeting with us and included a copy of *The Book of Alzheimer's For African American Congregations*. We heard back from him almost immediately with this very warm and gracious reply: "I pray this message finds you well. I received your letter and book regarding Alzheimer's as it relates to the African American context and was intrigued. I personally have had family members and former parishioners who struggle with the effects of Alzheimer's.

I would welcome an opportunity to chat further about your work and ministry. I would also like to introduce you to a few people in our senior adult ministry who might be interested in hearing more."

Shortly thereafter we visited with Dr. Cowser and one of his parishioners who was caring for an aunt with dementia. Dr. Cowser's beautiful collection of stoles he has been collecting since seminary were prominently displayed in his office. Seeing them and hearing him talk about them motivated me to follow through on my idea for the Alzheimer's Stole Ministry. It was only natural that he become one of the first recipients of a stole. When he received his stole in the mail he emailed me this note:

> How honored I felt this morning when I received the beautiful stole you created for me—a wonderful testimony and a reminder of those who suffer from Alzheimer's and those who care for them. The [Cynthia's] prayer was such a blessing. Thank you so much! I learned so much from you a few weeks ago and hope to connect to your ministry even more in the future. I would love for you to come and share with our Prime Timers Ministry sometime soon. I think it would be a wonderful opportunity to raise awareness and support in our congregation.

Shortly thereafter, we did visit his Prime Timers Ministry group where we talked about brain health and dementia, Don played his tenor banjo and sang some hymns with them, and they treated us to a tasty lunch. The Stole Ministry was working!

Rev. Dr. Dedric A. Cowser, United Methodist, Birmingham, AL

When Don and I visited with Pastors Derek Jacks and Sherrad Hayes at Homewood Cumberland Presbyterian Church in Birmingham, they invited us to have an information and fundraising table at their church's Annual Labor Day Barbecue and Yard Sale and set us up with a table at the front of the fellowship hall. Don brought some banjos to play music and I brought hand knit caps and blankets to sell. The sign Don made for our table said,

Talk to us about
Brain Health
Dementia
Caregiving
or Banjos!

We had lots of fun and lots of "takers" and I presented Pastor Derek with an Alzheimer's stole which he proudly wore over his chef's apron.

Rev. "Chef" Derek Jacks, Cumberland Presbyterian, Homewood, AL

I also made a stole for Associate Pastor Sherrad Hayes. They both chose to wear their stoles each Sunday in Advent for a month long campaign to raise awareness of the challenges faced by those living with dementia and their loved ones and to show their support as a dementia friendly faith community. Pastor Sherrad wrote this lovely reflection:

> I'm very grateful for the work you do raising awareness about Dementia and Alzheimer's. My paternal grandmother ("Nanny") had dementia at least the last year or so of her life. All of my other grandparents died when I was relatively young, between about 6 and 9 years old.

Nanny and I never lived more than a few miles apart from each other. So, I had a closer bond with her than any other grandparent. As she got progressively worse, she was placed in a nursing home next to the high school where I was a freshman. I have vivid memories of some of the last visits I had with her. She was in a completely different time and place. On some of the other visits, she thought I was my dad or my grandfather (who are also named "Sherrad"), but this time she recognized me. In her mind, I was much younger, and she was at her home. She smiled up at me and a few tears started to fall from her face. She began recounting memories of when I would spend the night at her house. She kept asking me when I was coming over to spend the night again. Not really knowing what to say, I told her, "Soon." She started talking about all the things we would do, and the TV shows we would watch, and what she would cook for us to eat. She was a wonderful cook. I stayed in that memory with her because it seemed to bring her some temporary peace and happiness. But in that moment, I felt mostly regret for not spending the night with her more often as I had gotten older. Soon after, she died.

My thoughts now are more of gratitude than regret, even though I do miss her. I can still taste her pancakes. I keep her well-worn Bible in my office. Today, I read a psalm she marked, Psalm 86 : "Bow down thine ear, O Lord, hear me: for I am poor and needy . . . But thou, O Lord, art a God full of compassion, and gracious, long suffering, and plenteous in mercy and truth."

In remembrance of his Nanny and Sherrad's gratitude for having had her in his life, his stole contains fabric with these words, "Gather together—give thanks—count your blessings."

Rev. Derek Jacks, Rev. Sherrad Hayes,
Cumberland Presbyterian, Homewood, AL and Lynda

Rev. Cynthia Abrams (October 11, 1960–January 11, 2019), Director, Health and Wholeness Program and Special Advisor to the General Secretary of the United Methodist Board of Church and Society, was a tireless advocate for the most vulnerable among us, and led us all with her extraordinary intelligence, energy, and compassion. Cynthia introduced UsAgainstAlzheimer's to the General Board of Church and Society resulting in the formation in 2015 of the Faith United Against Alzheimer's Coalition (FUAAC), a cooperative effort to mobilize all elements of the faith community in the fight against Alzheimer's disease and related dementias. Our coalition of faith based organizations continues to grow as we continually seek out and add other partners, including Volunteers of America, The Balm in Gilead, Dementia Friendly America, and Kingdom Mission Society. We believe that, together, we can and will make a difference on behalf of families facing dementia.

Just a few months before her death, at the 2018 UsAgainstAlzheimer's national summit, I presented this extraordinarily passionate advocate and worker for justice with an Alzheimer's stole. In her words,

> Clergy and congregations are on the front lines of this devastating disease, offering compassionate support to people who suffer from Alzheimer's and their families. The United Methodist Church has a long history of mobilizing, advocating and fundraising around many critical health and social justice issues; and we are anxious to do what we can to accelerate progress toward better treatments, prevention and a cure for Alzheimer's. My pastor's stole serves an an outward sign of this commitment.

We miss Cynthia and honor her memory by continuing her work.

CLERGY ADVOCATES

Rev. Cynthia Abrams, United Methodist, Manassas VA

Rev. Cynthia Huling Hummel visited us in October 2018. The pastors (Rev. Stephanie York Arnold, Rev. Katie Gilbert, and Rev. R.G. Wilson-Lyons) at First Church Birmingham (UMC) invited Cynthia to speak to a combined Sunday school class and to share with the full congregation during worship. They were doing a series of sermons based on one of Henri J. M. Nouwen's books, and that particular Sunday, the focus was on isolation/loneliness, a topic at the heart of dementia. I made and mailed them stoles in November as a thank you for hosting Cynthia. Stephanie sent us this reflection:

> This gift came at the perfect time. The week I received it we held a memorial service for a beloved member of our church who had lived with early onset dementia for

the last several years. We were able to ask the family if they would like us to wear our stoles during the service and use it as a time to draw attention to finding a cure for dementia and Alzheimer's, as well as supporting and walking with caregivers and family of those with these diseases. They were so honored for us to use the stoles in this way. It was a beautiful service in which their loved one's life was celebrated well and the community was in solidarity together. Thank you for giving us this opportunity through the gift of your presence and artistry!

Rev. Stephanie York Arnold, United Methodist, Birmingham, AL

Katie wrote:

>What a delight to come into the office to find a gift waiting on my desk! As I carefully unwrapped the paper, I was delighted to find a beautiful stole to reflect our work and learning on Alzheimer's. Only days before receiving the stole we received word that a long time member of

our congregation who had been suffering from early onset Alzheimer's had passed away. I knew immediately that the first place to use our stoles would be as part of his memorial service. And we did just that. The purple colors and ribbons on the stole remind us to honor his life by continuing our work and ministry to care, support, and love those facing Alzheimer's and other dementias.

Rev. Katie Gilbert, Cooperative Baptist Fellowship, Birmingham, AL

R.G. added his reflection, too:

> "How's school?" my grandmother had asked me for the fifth time in the last thirty minutes. I was 7 years old and my grandmother had been diagnosed with Alzheimer's for about a year. Over the next few years, in addition to asking the same questions, she began forgetting who people were, and, I'm sure out of frustration, easily lashed out in anger at people. I never really knew my

grandmother before her mind was affected by this terrible disease, but I've come to know the stories my dad tells. She was the first person to show up at a neighbor's or friend's house with a dish of food when they were in need. She was the last person to ever get angry. Her whole life had been taking care of other people. I never knew this version of my grandmother. I never knew who she truly was. Alzheimer's robbed that experience from me just as it robbed her of her memories, her mind, and even her temperament.

There are many reasons why I'm so grateful to be a part of this project. I've learned how to be a better minister to people who have Alzheimer's as well as to their caregivers. I've been able to help our congregation know how to respond in more helpful ways. But, like so many, I am grateful for this opportunity because my family has been personally affected.

Rev. R.G. Wilson-Lyons, United Methodist, Birmingham, AL

Pastor Paige Eaves' father had Amyotrophic lateral sclerosis (ALS), a progressive neurodegenerative disease that affects nerve cells in the brain and the spinal cord. ALS was first identified in 1869, but it wasn't until 1939 that Lou Gehrig brought national and international attention to the disease. Today one of the colors associated with the disease is blue and many advocates choose blue and white pin stripes to honor Lou Gehrig and others diagnosed with this disease. You'll note that I've incorporated lots of blue fabric and even some blue and white pin stripes in Pastor Paige's stole. Her husband's mother had Alzheimer's and she, too, was remembered as I made this stole. Upon receiving her stole, Paige sent this lovely thank you note:

> We [Paige and her husband, Forrest Robinson] are so touched by your beautiful letter and the gift of the stole and book [*Unmasking Alzheimer's*]. Your remembrance of the struggles of our parents is amazing to us. We are surprised, I think, at how deeply touched we are that you keep his mom and my dad in your hearts.

Pastor Paige Eaves and Forrest Robinson

Later she wrote this to share with our readers:

Stolen Memories

My grandmother died this year. She lived to 95—in her own home with her garden and her fabric arts and her antiques. Her heart kept beating through a lot of near misses, and then it simply gave out. We gathered around her in the hospital, where she was able to say goodbye and tell us where to find things. Hers is the kind of gracious life and death that we hope for ourselves and everyone we love.

However, this is not the story we can tell for my husband's mother, whose early-onset Alzheimer's stretched on for years as Forrest's sister struggled to care for her in Memphis. It is not the story we can tell for my stepfather, who died this year of dementia related to Parkinson's. And it is not the story of my father, who died at the age of 56 from ALS. These deaths were all extended and painful, stripping our loved ones of vitality and dignity, and re-ordering the lives of the family members who served as primary caregivers.

The more we have spoken of our experiences, the more we have realized that we are part of an all-too-large group of families affected by dementia and ALS. As a pastor, I have learned enough to know when to recommend that a family pursue a diagnosis. Even though a diagnosis of Alzheimer's or ALS will be bad news, that diagnosis puts a family in contact with a large network of medical and emotional support, and they won't be able to bear up without it.

We are grateful for the connection to the advocacy networks intent on ending Alzheimer's and ALS. Not only does it give us a way to act on our grief, but we have friends who remember our struggles and who keep our loved ones in their hearts.

This stole is weighty with the care and prayer that is sewn into it. I look forward to wearing it as a way to increase awareness of Alzheimer's and ALS. You will see from the photo that my stole has blue ALS advocacy colors sewn into it. My congregation will be so appreciative and will want to know more.

We are proud to be part of the extended circle of supporters and advocates.

Rev. Paige Eaves, United Methodist, LaMirada, CA

I met Pastor Bobby Fields on the bus to Nashville in 2009 on my first ever advocacy trip. Within minutes of our meeting he began calling me "Mom" and he became my "Tennessee son." He was the Program Director for Alzheimer's Tennessee but most importantly, he became "family" during the last years of my late husband Richard's life. He walked with me during this most difficult time and we shared tears, worries, but also laughter. It was a joy to make a stole for Bobby and he wrote this loving reply:

> The stole is beautiful . . . I promptly wore my stole the first Sunday after I received it. After receiving the compliments from church members, I explained its meaning and personal significance from the pulpit. I remember my grandmother's battle with dementia and my 13 ½ years working with a nonprofit Alzheimer's organization. I will continue to wear my stole and, as I remind people of what God, through Jesus, by way of His Holy Spirit did for us, I will also keep in our remembrance those that

are now living and have lived with dementia, and what great things we can do to love, care for and support those currently afflicted.

"And now faith, hope and love abide, these three; and the greatest of these is love."

–1 Corinthians 13:13 (NRSV)

Rev. Bobby Fields, Jr., Baptist, Maryville, TN

Kathy Fogg Berry's DVD and Study Guide, *When Words Fail: Practical Ministry to People with Dementia and Their Caregivers,* was one of the many excellent resources we provided to pastors on our visits. All too often, as memories and abilities fade and the capacity to communicate weakens, those with dementia and their caregivers find themselves neglected or forgotten by the larger community. Despite good intentions, when words begin to fail for people with dementia, words also fail for those around them, who don't know what to say or what to do. Kathy's DVD is filled with teaching, demonstrations of effective ministry, and inspiring ways to bring joy and spiritual nourishment to people living with dementia and their care partners. The musical notations in Kathy's stole are intended to honor her late grandmother-in-law and her mother-in-law, both of whom had/have dementia. Upon receiving her stole, Kathy wrote:

> My grandmother-in-law taught piano for over 50 years and my mother-in-law played piano and sang beautifully. Connecting through singing, on good days, is still something we enjoy doing together. When Evelyn sings, her face transforms from worry to warmth. Anxiety lines disappear, and her eyes open as the words of old, traditional hymns seem to wash clouds of confusion away. For the last 18 years since my mother-in-law's Alzheimer's diagnosis, music has remained her best connection to an overwhelming world. The same remained true for her mother, Ola, who also knew dementia too well. A piano teacher for more than 50 years, Ola retained her love of music and found peace in its power until the day she died.
>
> When Lynda offered to create a beautiful stole to thank me for serving as a memory support chaplain and to honor my loved ones, I knew it had to depict music. Dementia cannot quench the soul's song. This stole is a precious reminder of that.

Stolen Memories

Rev. Kathy Fogg Berry, Interdenominational Christian, Richmond, VA

Shortly after our having met Rev. Jason Carson Wilson at the UsA2 summit, I phoned him to offer an individualized stole to use in his advocacy as a self-proclaimed "angelic troublemaker." He gave me several ideas for fabric designs that would honor his loved ones with dementia. Several weeks later he wore his new stole at his ordination and sent us this reflection:

> Ordained ministry is at once a privilege and a burden. Being invited into people's lives in both joyous and sorrow-filled times is a privilege. Celebrating their joys is no problem. Carrying people's sorrows—which ministers often wish they could lift—can be burdensome.
>
> Stoles embody the juxtaposition of ministry's privilege and burden. Even wearing a stole, while still a licensed (not-yet-ordained) United Church of Christ minister, this faith leader felt its weight. And my woven

rainbow-themed stole added a few pounds. It represents a marginalized community held dear, my denomination's commitment to creating a just world for all, and the belief that my social justice ministry continues Jesus' ministry to and for the oppressed.

My new ClergyAgainstAlzheimer's stole gives a different vibe. It also represents ministry's awesome responsibility, and its panels shroud this minister with ancestors' and elders' love and support. The purple ribbons, rainbow, and cross blocks symbolize the obvious. Those sewing machine blocks pay homage to my great-grandmother, Lucille Mae Denniston Wilson Harrington, who raised me. She succumbed to Alzheimer's in Champaign, IL on April 19, 2009.

Grandma taught me to read. She provided a safe space, where a little Black gay boy could be himself. And, Grandma shielded me from alcoholism and child abuse. She helped give me confidence to realize more than one dream. That confidence allowed me to navigate my way through the University of Illinois at Urbana-Champaign's College of Media (then College of Communications), where this future minister and policy advocate earned a print journalism degree. That degree launched a journalism career that strangely prepared me for ministry. Wearing Lynda's ministerial masterpiece keeps Grandma close to my heart. My future and past careers would help forge a bond between me and Greg O'Brien, affectionately known as "the poet laureate of Alzheimer's." Greg has been living with Alzheimer's since 2009 and continues to share his journey with candor, courage and faith. The typewriter block represents that bond.

Although I'm an ordained United Church of Christ minister, I serve as Minister of Liberation Formation at Metropolitan Community Church of Washington, DC (MCCDC). Grandma and spirits of LGBTQIA ancestors surrounded me during a ceremony blessing my service there—and during my first sermon.

Wearing that stole, of course, draws me close to God and reminds me of promises made during my Nov. 4, 2018 ordination service at University Church (UChurch), a United Church of Christ/Disciples of

Christ congregation in Hyde Park, Chicago. I serve as its Minister of Social Justice Education and Advocacy; but, I've been deployed to Washington, DC.

The vow to accept the privilege and burden to celebrate joys or stand with people in sorrow is made tangible, thanks to the stole. Lynda's stole embodies those I love and respect, who cloak me with comfort and support when times get difficult. That comfort and support sustains me as I continue doing the work that the United Church of Christ, Justice & Witness Ministries' Washington, DC office allowed me to begin. It sustains me as I serve MCCDC and UChurch, but also as I work to grow my nonprofit, Bayard Rustin Liberation Initiative (BRLI). BRLI is dedicated to helping create a just world for LGBTQIA people and people of color through "angelic troublemaking" for justice. Lynda's masterpiece gives me comfort and courage, while symbolizing the profound commitment ministry requires.

Rev. Jason Carson Wilson, United Church of Christ, Washington, DC

CLERGY ADVOCATES

Closeup of Jason's Stole

Rev. Amy Rollins Probst's stole includes fabric with blue stars and red stripes. When Richard died, I had a memorial service for him that was wonderfully attended, but decided to have a private burial at a rural veterans' cemetery as I felt that would best honor who he was. He had served in the Marine Corps for only 4 years when he was 17–21, but, "once a Marine, always a Marine." He loved the simple beauty of the East Tennessee countryside (He called it "God's country.") and he had been raised in a very rural community. The only people in attendance were me, Amy, my pastor Brenda Carroll, my friend Ginny West Case, and two young Marines who played Taps and folded the flag on Richard's coffin to give to me. The memory that is seared in my mind is the picture of our hands laid together upon the coffin as Amy and Brenda prayed our goodbyes. The love and support of these three women meant so much to me. I hoped that the stars and stripes and the churches in the rural setting would remind Amy of that day and all whom she has attended who have been touched by Alzheimer's. It was in writing these words that it dawned on me that the Alzheimer's Stole Ministry was—as the expressive arts often do—ministering to me! "For it is in giving that we receive . . ." (St. Francis of Assisi)

Upon receiving her stole, Amy sent me this message, "I wanted to tell you that I received the package you sent and I wept. It might have been one of the most thoughtful gifts I have ever received." When I asked her to share a reflection for this book, she wrote:

> For over twenty years I've been blessed and humbled to serve as a pastor. Throughout that time, I have journeyed with a number of people at various stages of many diseases. The diseases of the mind, however, are a special kind of hell. For those who are trapped within bodies that are strong or deteriorating, knowing that they are losing themselves—or not understanding at all what is happening—this must be some of the very definition of hell. For separation from our Divine Creator is that ultimate place or relationship of void, abysmal despair, vast nothingness. This is hell. The blessed gift of hope is that our Divine One is still present, even in this despairing time. The juxtaposition of the "already and the not yet" of living through some of the darkest days while at the same time having the opportunity for the closest embrace of the One who Created and Sustains us can be either crazy making or offer abiding peace (Or for many of us, both, depending on the day and moment!). For those who care for loved ones along this journey, who lose them not once, but over and over, this too is a tortuous existence.
>
> That is why I wear this beautiful stole in front of the "Laughing Jesus." This stole was an amazingly beautiful and generous gift from my friend Lynda reminding me of the day in the spring of 2012 when we stood together, holding hands, to say a final goodbye to her dear husband

Richard. I was privileged to stand with her as an invited guest in a rural military cemetery in East Tennessee in that special moment of remembering. In the years since, I have looked on with awe as Lynda has turned "mourning into dancing" again and again—refusing to be relegated into a hell of loss, loneliness and hopelessness.

Now in my own days, as my journey leads me down the unpredicted and unpredictable path of being a caregiver for my own dear husband, also a proud retired member of the military, I look up. I wear this stole today for hope. I wear this stole for community. I wear this stole in honor of my husband and all who suffer. I also wear it in honor of the one who has taught me and is teaching me to not allow this journey to steal your essence, but to look for the glimpses of Heaven. Lynda, as one who walked this path with her dad and her spouse, and as an advocate and spokesperson for those with dementia and their loved ones, continues to affirm for me what it is to walk with Hope. As I watch her, I am inspired and reminded that the loss of cognition may diminish us physically but not spiritually for, whatever happens, nothing, not even dementia, can steal personhood. And as I listen, I see glimpses of the One who first bound us closely together and who undergirds both of us with a strength beyond ourselves. This One, the Divine, points us to Heaven and the powerful words of one of my favorite verses of scripture, true for all people in all seasons, Psalm 139: 7-14 (NIV):

> Where can I go from your Spirit?
> Where can I flee from your presence?
> If I go up to the heavens, you are there;
> if I make my bed in the depths, you are there.
> If I rise on the wings of the dawn,
> if I settle on the far side of the sea,
> even there your hand will guide me,
> your right hand will hold me fast.
> If I say, "Surely the darkness will hide me
> and the light become night around me,"

even the darkness will not be dark to you;
the night will shine like the day,
for darkness is as light to you.
For you created my inmost being;
you knit me together in my mother's womb.
I praise you because I am fearfully and wonderfully made.

Rev. Amy Rollins Probst, United Methodist, Kingsport, TN

We met Rev. Danielle Thompson when she and her fellow Episcopalian priests hosted a workshop to educate their congregations about dementia and the demands of caregiving. Danielle graciously invited us to lunch to discuss ways in which her congregation could expand its ministry of advocacy and support for those in our community facing dementia. After our visit I made an Alzheimer's stole for Danielle.

Shortly thereafter, during an evening worship service, Danielle spoke to her congregation about the call to walk beside those impacted by dementia. She then held up her new stole, blessed it, removed the one she was wearing and replaced it with her Alzheimer's stole as a symbol of her congregation's call and answer to serve this special ministry of remembrance. It was truly a sacred moment. When I shared this with Cynthia Huling Hummel it caused another "Aha" moment. We realized that the blessing was not "just" for the pastor; it was a blessing and an exhortation for the whole community of faith. It occurred to us that other pastors may wish to consecrate their stoles and their ministry as Danielle had done so beautifully. With this is mind, Cynthia wrote an expanded stole blessing:

> A Special Blessing for An Alzheimer's Stole
> and for Clergy and Congregations
> By Rev. Dr. Cynthia Huling Hummel
>
> God of Blessings, We ask that you bless this stole, that you bless the one who wears it and that you bless this community of faith as they answer your call to serve your beloved people: those with Alzheimer's and related dementias. We pray this day for those whose memories are fading, especially for those who feel lost and alone and for those who have forgotten who they are and whose they are. Thank you for calling (insert name of clergy/faith leader) and (insert name of congregation) to this special ministry of remembrance.
> Calling One: You have called _____ to walk beside care partners, family, and friends on this difficult and challenging journey and we thank you this day for the "care-ers" in our lives and for their ministry of presence.
> Faithful One: You have called _____ not only to teach and preach your holy Word, but also to challenge people to live as your faithful followers who share and show YOUR love to those living with Alzheimer's and other dementias. We thank you for calling _____ to this ministry of inclusion.

Healing God: Give _____ strength and courage for the journey ahead as she/he tends to those whose hearts and dreams are shattered by this disease and as she/he reminds us all that you will never leave us or forsake us, but that you walk beside us in times of pain, sorrow and joy. Tears may linger through the night, but joy will come in the morning.

Creator God: Just as this Alzheimer's stole was stitched together from many pieces of fabric, bring us together into a new creation: united in our shared hope of a world without Alzheimer's. We join hearts and voices in prayer for researchers who are searching for a cure, working on treatments, and developing interventions. We thank you, too, for the advocates who are raising awareness and for their devotion to their tasks.

Gathering God, We thank you for this community of faith: for those who have heard, responded to and embraced Your call to this special ministry of being present to those who have Alzheimer's and related dementias. Bless these helpers who touch hearts and lives in meaningful moments. Bless those who share in respite care. Bless those who tell stories and sing songs, those who join in making art with heart, and those who guide and reminisce as they share Your abiding love.

Remembering One: We know that you will never forget us for YOU have written our names on the palm of Your hand and hold us close to Your heart. So please dear Lord, bless this stole, bless the one who wears it and bless all in this place who have answered Your call to serve. Thank you, Lord. Amen.

Rev. Danielle Thompson, Episcopalian, Birmingham, AL

We remember Rev. Carol Steinbrecher's dad, who had dementia, with the tools placed on the left side of her stole over her heart. "He was very handy around the house: he could fix and repair almost everything." Here is her reflection:

> We come to Christ's table and Jesus says, "Remember. Remember me." As caretakers for those with Alzheimers, part of the pain of this disease is watching our loved ones lose their precious memories bit by bit. So we become the keepers of their stories. We come laden with photo albums and mementos, and we remember for them. Jesus says, "Come unto me you who are heavy laden and I will give you rest." Those with Alzheimer's join with Jesus in saying, "Remember me. Remember *for* me."

Rev. Carol Steinbrecher, Congregational Church, Sharon, MA

CLERGY ADVOCATES

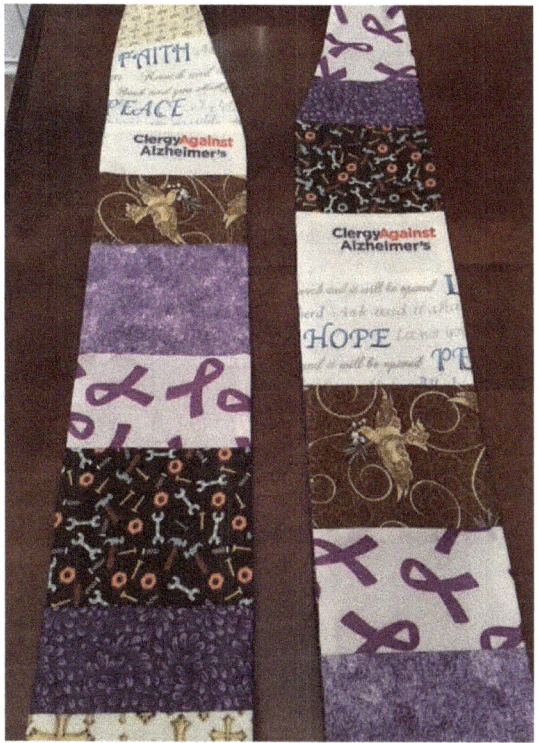

Detail of Rev. Carol's Stole

When we visited with Rev. Julie Conrady, the pastor of the Universal Unitarian Church of Birmingham, she shared that her grandmother had had dementia and she was eager to educate her congregation on caring for those affected by dementia. She invited us to speak to her congregation about brain health during an upcoming service, which is one of the goals of our dementia friendly faith communities initiative. Her faith tradition is not credal and the use of any particular religious symbols that were clearly Christian or Jewish, etc. would not be appropriate. However, we were able to find fabric online that had the most widely used symbol of her faith, the flaming chalice. I also used some forget-me-not flowers fabric as they are a symbol of remembrance and Julie's grandmother had been especially fond of flowers.

Rev. Julie Conrady, Universal Unitarian, Birmingham, AL

Rev. Dr. Dwyn Mounger is a lifelong advocate for people affected by dementia, a member of ClergyAgainstAlzheimer's, and a close friend of Richard Morgan. And, he loves stoles. So, it was an honor to make him a stole. He honored us even more with these words:

> Throughout my ministry of 50-plus years I've been very much aware of how basic elements of common Christian worship—the unison Lord's Prayer/Our Father, a traditional hymn, the Apostles' Creed, the bread and wine of Holy Communion, the unison 23rd Psalm in the King James version—can be, by the Holy Spirit, bridges across the deep valleys of even the worst depths of dementia.

And I have seen visiting, praying with, and especially celebrating the Lord's Supper with those seemingly lost in Alzheimer's, as a major part of my calling to ministry. A 30-minute Communion service in a nursing home, with the basic liturgical elements, can bring out surprisingly enthusiastic responses from a congregation large or small in size. It's heretical to think—as, sadly, some clergy seem to do—that the sacraments are reserved just for those believers who can "understand" and grasp them intellectually! Even that Sorbonne & Orleans-educated philosopher/lawyer/theologian Calvin, when it came to the Eucharist, figuratively threw down his ceaseless pen, and confessed, "I rather experience than understand it!"

During the past 30 years or so I've found, too, how powerful, soothing, and, yes, healing, brief services of wholeness, including prayers and anointing with oil—making the sign of the cross with one's thumb on the forehead of the ill—can be, and I practice this regularly in the congregations I've served.

Now, as the grateful owner of one of Lynda's beautiful stoles, I plan to wear it regularly in my new—and probably last—part-time interim pastorate that I recently began here in East Tennessee. Not only will I wear this stole, I will also appeal to other ordained ministers and elders to volunteer to accompany me on visits to those in our congregation who face the challenges of this disease.

Stolen Memories

Rev. Dr. Dwyn Mounger, Presbyterian (USA), Maryville, TN

Another Alzheimer's advocate and founding member of ClergyAgainstAlzheimer's, Rev. Dr. Steven Eason, lives just down the road from Dwyn in Knoxville, TN. He is a much published Christian author and he offered this reflection upon receiving his stole:

> A pastor's stole. Stolen Memories. I am struck by the play on words. It feels as if something, or someone "stole" my mother. She was diagnosed with Alzheimer's in the early 1990s and passed away in 2005. She left in stages. Alzheimer's feels like a thief has come into your home and stolen your loved one. Where did they go? How do we relate to who is left? She was a different person in many ways, and yet the same. She was still my mother.

Sometimes when people steal something, they give it back. It's rare. Our faith, our hope, our love longs for God to give our loved ones back. That doesn't happen in this life. What a wonderful thing it will be if it happens in the next!

Rev. Dr. Steven Eason, Presbyterian (USA), Knoxville, TN

What began as a Christian Alzheimer's Stole Ministry expanded when our friend Rabbi Steve Glazer asked if I could sew him a tallit for his use in advocacy as a rabbi. He explained that some tallitot or prayer shawls are very similar in design and use to a stole, not surprising as they are probably its ancestor. Like stoles, they are made in a number of different styles and dimensions and have many different fabrics and symbols added to create very individualized pieces of religious art. For example, I made Steve a tallit that flares gently the whole length and has various Jewish symbols such as a menorah, peace doves, Hebrew letters, and the Star of David.

However, a tallit does differ from a stole in that it has twined and knotted fringes called tzitzit at the four corners of the bottom. These have special meaning and significance as Steve explained to us: "The knotted fringes are what a scholar decades ago referred to as 'ritual macrame.' They must be wrapped and knotted in a very specific way so that the total of turns plus knots of all four add up to 613, the number of commandments in Jewish tradition. The origin is Numbers 15:37–41, and seeing them is a visual reminder of the commandments." The wearer usually ties their own directly onto the tallit.

We eventually learned that tallitot come in many styles and designs that vary tremendously according to particular cultural, ethnic and religious branches, movements or streams of Jewish traditions. In some of these the tallit is worn by lay men as well as rabbis or even by women in others. In some, the tallit may be worn underneath an outer garment with the fringe showing beneath. The important core is in the meaning, especially that of the tzizit. Tallitot are frequently stored and transported in their own bags, which share the importance of the artistic design and symbols in remembrance of the commandments. These bags are simple to make but are also available online.

We had lots of communication with Steve during the planning and construction of his tallit. He thanked me many times and told me, "I'm really excited that you're willing to make me one, and I know that I shall love it and wear it proudly. I am hoping it will also provide an opportunity to do a lot of educating, both about Alzheimer's and the work of UsAgainstAlzheimer's!"

CLERGY ADVOCATES

Rabbi Steven M. Glazer, Jewish, N. Bethesda, MD

Rabbi Dr. Oren Steinitz is the spiritual leader of Congregation Kol Ami in Elmira, NY and a friend of Rev. Dr. Cynthia Huling Hummel. She met Rabbi Oren when she moved to Elmira in 2011 after her diagnosis of amnestic mild cognitive impairment and was invited by a friend to attend a Shabbat service at the synagogue. She was warmly welcomed by Rabbi Oren and his congregation and now regularly attends Shabbat services and other events at the synagogue. Cynthia wanted to thank Rabbi Oren and his congregation for their ongoing support, prayers and interest in truly becoming a dementia friendly faith community by presenting Rabbi Oren with an Alzheimer's tallit at a Friday night Shabbat service. It was an honor to make one for her to give to him. Here is Rabbi Oren's reflection:

Stolen Memories

Jewish tradition seems to be overtly focused on memory and remembering. The first blessing of the Amidah, our central prayer, refers to God as the One "who remembers the merits of our ancestors." The Shabbat liturgy tells us that the Sabbath serves as a double reminder: it was instituted in memory of the Exodus from Egypt as well as in memory of the work of creation; Rosh HaShannah is referred to in the liturgy as the Day of Remembrance, and we spend one of its main liturgical units on Zichronot, the biblical verses concerning memory and remembering. There are, of course, many more examples.

The emphasis on memory is not coincidental. Benedict Anderson, a political scientist and historian best known for his book, *Imagined Communities*, wrote that memory is one of the main vehicles of forming a national identity. In other words, a nation, or any large community, cannot be formed without collective memories. We simply cannot feel close to other people in a group, if we do not share memories with them. Just like our personal families are strengthened by creating memories, both positive and negative, Judaism is built on the idea that all of us, collectively, remember certain events. While a Jew who lives in Elmira does not necessarily have that much in common with a Jew living in Brazil or Singapore, both of them "remember" that many years ago, their ancestors were slaves in Egypt and God brought them out of there to freedom.

If memories create our identity, then what happens to us when we start losing our memories? Oftentimes, those living with Alzheimer's or other dementias feel like their identity is slowly drifting away from them. So often we hear from those suffering from dementia "I don't know who I am anymore." Without remembering our memories, we lose our connection to our families, to our communities, and even to ourselves.

The Torah tells us that the reason we are to wear tsitsit is that we "may remember, and do all of [God's] commandments." The wonderful tallit that Lynda designed serves as a powerful reminder of those whose memories are drifting from them. It is a reminder to us to love our neighbors as ourselves, especially when our neighbors struggle to find their place in our communities and the world.

I am so grateful to Lynda for this wonderful gift.

Rabbi Dr. Oren Steinitz, Jewish, Elmira, NY

Rabbi Israel de la Piedra serves as the Director of Spiritual Care for the Miami Jewish Health Systems. In addition to offering pastoral care to residents and patients of all backgrounds, he leads the Shabbat service for the residents affected by dementia every Friday afternoon. He wrote a very helpful and informative chapter about this service for *Dementia-friendly Worship* so I wrote to ask if he might like to have an Alzheimer's tallit. When he shared with me the parameters for a tallit that he was familiar with, regretfully, I had to reply as follows: "I am so sorry but I am afraid that the type of tallit that you describe is beyond my expertise and ability. The pastors' stoles and Rabbi Steve's tallit are all quite simple and much smaller—about 4-1/2 inches wide at the neck and Steve's gently flares to about 8 inches at the bottom. The others do not widen out. The only tallit I know how to make is a stole style tallit."

Rabbi Israel responded that he very much wanted to be a part of this project and requested a tallit like the one I made for Rabbi Steve, "It will be my special tallit for the service I do for our residents with dementia, the service I wrote about for the book. Currently I don't wear a tallit for that service, but if you go ahead and send me one just like the one Rabbi Steve has, that will be my very special tallit for that service, and I will be so proud to wear it in that special setting."

Upon receiving his tallit, he wrote this lovely reflection:

My Very Special Tallit

When I was contacted by Lynda Everman to ask me if I would want to have a tallit—the ritual Jewish prayer shawl—as part of the work she was doing on stoles, I responded quite enthusiastically. I wrote back to her and said that I would love to be part of this sacred initiative, and then proceeded to give her the requirements of a tallit. I said that it should be wide enough for me to wrap myself with it, it should preferably be white and blue, and so on. Lynda responded thanking me for my interest but told me that unfortunately she could not make such a tallit, but only one that was an enlarged version of the stoles she had been making.

Lynda's answer left me sad and disappointed with myself. How could I have the chutzpah to ask for something different from what I had been so kindly offered? How could I let the opportunity to make a meaningful statement about caring for people with dementia go by?

Life for those affected by dementia is one of constant contradictions, a life where what was and what is exist simultaneously in a tense struggle for the soul of the person. Those who are affected by dementia continue to live in the same world they have always lived in, continue to have the same body they have always had, continue to be surrounded by their same loved ones, continue to be the same human being they have always been. But just as everything stays the same, nothing is really the same: their world looks different, their body is not under their full control, they are surrounded by people they do not know or do not recognize, their sense of their humanity has changed. This paradox of being the same human being they have always been while at the same time being a different person in so many ways is what makes dementia such a hard thing to face—for both the person with dementia as well as for their loved ones.

That is when I understood what this tallit that Lynda was offering me meant, and why it would be such a strong messenger of the holiness that I try to share with the residents suffering from dementia as we pray together in our weekly Shabbat service. My new tallit looks very different from what I have always thought of as a tallit. But at the same time my new tallit is a tallit just like any other tallit I have ever had. My new tallit would at the same time be different and similar to every other tallit—just as dementia makes us different in so many ways from whom we were and yet we remain the same person we have always been.

My new tallit does not wrap around me like a regular tallit. My new tallit is skinny rather than wide. My new tallit has very little white on it rather than being a white garment. My new tallit looks so different from the four or five other ones that I own. And yet, it is a tallit by all the requirements of Jewish law: it has four corners, and it allows me to hang my tzitzit—the tassels, or ritual fringes—from it.

When I wear my new tallit during Shabbat services I will not be wrapped around by it, but I will feel the love and the prayers and the singing and the eyes of those present wrapping around me, providing me with more of a sense of warmth and belonging than any garment around my shoulders and over my back could ever give me.

But that is not all. The tallit's role is just to be a hanger really, a four-cornered garment from which to hang the tzitzit. The Torah commands us to wear the tzitzit so that, as we say every day during the Shema prayer, "you shall see [the tzitzit] and remember all the commandments of the Lord" (Numbers 15:39). And so, every time I will don my special tallit, I will see the tzitzit that hang from it and will remember the commandments—including the central commandment of the Jewish faith, as explained by the Talmudic sage Hillel, "What is hateful to you, to your fellow don't do. That's the entirety of the Torah; everything else is elaboration." (Shabbat 31a)

The verse from Numbers cited above goes on, however. It is not enough to just remember the commandments when we see the tzitzit: the Torah goes on to say that the reason we must remember the commandments when we see the tzitzit is to "perform them." And so, I will always see my special tallit as a call to treat others as I want to be treated myself—as I want to be treated now and as I want to be treated the day when I cannot take care of myself anymore. My special tallit is a holy object not because it still complies with the technical requirements for a tallit—those requirements just make this particular garment a tallit. Rather, my special tallit is a holy object because it is a call to holy action, a call to take care of our fellow human beings no matter how much they are changing, no matter how difficult it is for them to ask for what they need, no matter how difficult it is for them to go on living.

Thank you, Lynda. This special tallit has helped me to open my eyes to see how we are always the same, no matter how much we might change as dementia takes over. I will remember this lesson every Friday afternoon, as I don my special tallit for the Shabbat service with our residents with dementia.

God bless you and all those who work to make life better for those with dementia.

CLERGY ADVOCATES

Rabbi Israel de la Piedra, Jewish, Miami, FL

When Rev. Cynthia Huling Hummel presented Rabbi Oren Steinitz with his tallit, her friend and fellow Fire Chaplain Bill Mayo commented on how much he liked it and asked how he could get one. Bill is the Chief Chaplain for the New York State Association of Fire Chaplains (NYSAFC) and thought that wearing an Alzheimer's tallit would provide a great opportunity to further educate the NYSAFC—and all first responders—about becoming dementia friendly. This is his reflection:

> The 23rd Psalm reminds us of God's presence in times of difficulty. I am a Fire Chaplain for the Plainview, NY Fire Department, and serve as the Chief Chaplain for the New York State Association of Fire Chaplains. Fire chaplains show up to provide spiritual support and comfort to individuals and families who are dealing with a crisis situation. We respond to fires, car accidents, missing person reports, hazardous materials incidents, and much more.

We are there not just to provide support to those directly involved in the accident or incident; we also support the helpers on the scene: our fellow firefighters, EMTs, and police. Fire chaplains provide a faithful presence in times of uncertainty to people of all faiths. We listen. We care. We share God's love.

Alzheimer's is like a blazing fire that is spreading across our country. Nearly 5.8 million Americans are living with Alzheimer's or a related dementia, and so many of our family members, friends, and neighbors are affected. On behalf of our organization, I am proud to say that we have had, and we continue to offer, dementia specific training and resources to our chaplains across our great state of New York, so that we are better equipped to help individuals and families who might need our assistance. An example of this might be responding to an "alert" for someone with a memory impairment who is lost or wandering and knowing how we might help.

It is an honor to wear this tallit, that shows my personal support and NYSAFC's support for those living with Alzheimer's and related dementias, their care partners, family and friends. By serving others we are serving our God.

Chief Chaplain William Mayo, Jewish, Plainview, NY

6

Instructions

A. WHAT YOU'LL NEED TO GET STARTED

Tools and Supplies:

simple sewing machine—you only have to know how to sew a straight line

> walking foot—this prevents shifting and puckering that may occur with a normal presser foot and makes sewing multiple layers easier because the presser foot on top of your fabric moves (or walks) at the same pace that your machine's feed dogs are moving the bottom layer of fabric
>
> self healing cutting mat—24" x 36"
>
> rotary cutter and lots of sharp blades
>
> sharp scissors
>
> quilter's ruler
>
> quilter's pins
>
> small post-it notes for labeling and numbering pieces

iron, ironing board

clear starch and sizing alternative—I use Mary Ellen's Best Press (800-328-6294—maryellenproducts.com)

no-show mesh stabilizer—I like the 12" x 10 yard roll from Nancy's Notions (800-833-0690—nancysnotions.com)

Of course, thread

And, then there's the fabric!

Fabric for Front of the Stole or Tallit

Purple ribbons—I found Alzheimer's Awareness bandanas at Oriental Trading Company (800-875-8480 orientaltrading.com). I usually repeat this fabric and try to keep the overall color scheme predominately purple (widely accepted as the color for Alzheimer's awareness). Tallitot often have a lot of blue colors in them, too, or sometimes the traditional white background, but there are no absolute rules. The important thing here is the tzitzit fringe so I would check with the intended wearer as to their personal preferences for colors and symbols.

Religious symbols or words appropriate to the faith tradition

Forget-me-not fabric (forget-me-not flowers are often used as symbols for undying love, remembrance, a connection that lasts through time despite separation or other challenges, and memories)

Maybe fabric that represents something you've learned about the clergy member or their loved one with dementia

If it's not going to be a surprise, or even if it is and you can get a family member in on it, you can ask for ties, pretty handkerchiefs, or clothing from loved ones who had dementia—the only requirement is that you are able to cut a piece of fabric from it that's 5" by 5" for a stole or 5" by 8-1/2" for a tallit.

Hobby Lobby (hobbylobby.com) often has religious themed fabric. There are many choices online. I've often found fabric on Etsy (etsy.com). If you're already a quilter, look in your stash. Mix

INSTRUCTIONS

and match your fabrics—corduroy, cotton, polyester is okay too. Batiks and brocades are wonderful. While you don't need a lot of each fabric (more on that further down) you will need about 10–11 different fabrics for your stole. If you are purchasing fabric for your stole, buy 1/6 of a yard (6" x width of fabric) of each fabric for the front of the stole. (That extra inch allows you to straighten the fabric if you need to.)

Fabric for Back of the Stole or Tallit

I typically use purple fabric for the back of each stole or tallit. Buy at least 1/2 yard (18" x width of fabric). You won't need quite this much for the back of a stole but this will allow you to have several pieces of this fabric on the front as well. Cut the fabric in long strips that are 5" x width of the fabric (generally about 42") for a stole or 8-1/2" for a tallit x width of fabric.

Tips on Construction

You can't pin too much or press too often.

After experimenting with my first stoles, I decided that I liked having the 2 bottom pieces each be 5" tall. I also like to use a little of the back material on the front of the stole. You just don't want to place it at the bottom of the stole as you're going to create about a 1" hem with the backing material and it's nice to have a "contrasting" hem.

Be creative: some people might add fringe to the bottom or sew on special buttons (e.g. forget-me-not flowers) or embroider designs (e.g. cross, dove, fish, etc.). You might even wish to quilt your stole.

B. HOW TO MAKE A BASIC STOLE

The following instructions will produce a stole that is approximately 4-1/2" wide by 86-88" long.

Stolen Memories

Assemble your fabrics. As stated above, I like to use about 10–11 different fabrics in each stole. The individual pieces of fabric are all cut 5" wide and heights of either 2-1/2", 4", or 5" tall. Cut:

9 each 2-1/2"
10 each 4"
8 each 5"

As you cut your pieces, lay them out in two vertical rows, putting 4 each of the 2-1/2" pieces, 5 each of the 4" pieces, and 4 each of the 5" pieces in each row. You will have one 2-1/2" piece left over. That is the "connector"—also the center back of the stole. When you finish laying the fabric pieces out, you will have 2 equal lengths of about 50 inches long before sewing and one 2-1/2" "connector" in the center back.

Now label and number your pieces so that when you pick them up, you will have them in the proper order for sewing. For example:

1—Left side as you're facing it
2
3 . . .
1—Right side as you're facing it
2
3 . . .

The pieces in the following picture are color-coded to illustrate how I arranged the different sized pieces in this particular stole:

9 each 2-1/2"—yellow post-it
10 each 4"—pink post-it
8 each 5"—gold post-it

Instructions

Cut one length of the no-show mesh stabilizer about 45" long and then cut it in half the long way so you have two "facings" that are 6" wide and 45" long.

All seams are 1/4 inch. (I don't really measure my seam allowances; I simply use the edge of my walking foot as a guide. That's close enough!)

Sew from edge of stabilizer.

Trim excess facing.

    Sew both sides of the front together at the neck. Mark center.

    Now cut strips of fabric 5" wide to make your backing. You will need the length of your finished stole + about 2–1/2" more at the lower edge of each side for the hem. If you have to piece the fabric to make it long enough (and you probably will), add the extra length to the middle of the stole. Also, when calculating the finished length of fabric you will need, be sure to account for seam allowances each time you piece the fabric.

Starting at the center of the front and back sides, pin both sides together with the right sides of the fabric facing each other. Sew each of the two long sides from the center out. Sew one side all the way. On the other side, leave about 6–7" in the center open so you can turn the stole right side out. Leave the lower edges (ends) open.

Turn the stole right side out and hand stitch the center to close it. Use a "slip stitch" or "blind stitch" to make it as invisible as possible. Then hem each end with the extra fabric from the back of the stole. Again, create a blind stitch by hand.

C. STEPPING UP TO A CONTOURED NECKLINE

As above, the following instructions will produce a stole that is approximately 4–1/2" wide by 86–88" long.

Assemble your fabrics. The individual pieces of fabric are all cut 5" wide and heights of either 2–1/2", 4", 5", or 6" tall. Cut:

8 each 2–1/2"
10 each 4"
6 each 5"
2 each 6"

As you cut your pieces, lay them out in two vertical rows, placing the two 6" pieces at the top of each row, then put 4 each of the 2–1/2" pieces, 5 each of the 4" pieces, and 3 each of the 5" pieces in each row. As above, I like to end with a 5" piece at the bottom of each row.

Now label and number your pieces so that when you pick them up, you will have them in the proper order for sewing.

The pieces in the following picture are color-coded as follows:

8 each 2–1/2"—yellow post-it
10 each 4"—pink post-it
6 each 5"—gold post-it
2 each 6"—purple post-it

Instructions

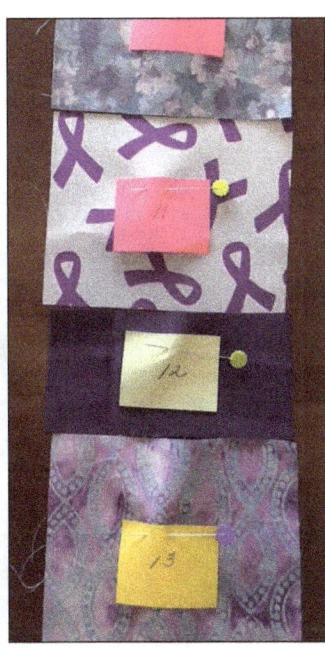

Cut one length of the no-show mesh stabilizer about 45" long and then cut it in half the long way so you have two "facings" that are 6" wide and 45" long.

As above, sew from edge where fabric and stabilizer meet.

STOLEN MEMORIES

Trim excess facing.

    At this point you need to make a template or neck pattern for the contour. You can make one or two identical templates. If you make just one, you will need to flip it for the opposite side so that it faces correctly on the stole.

Instructions

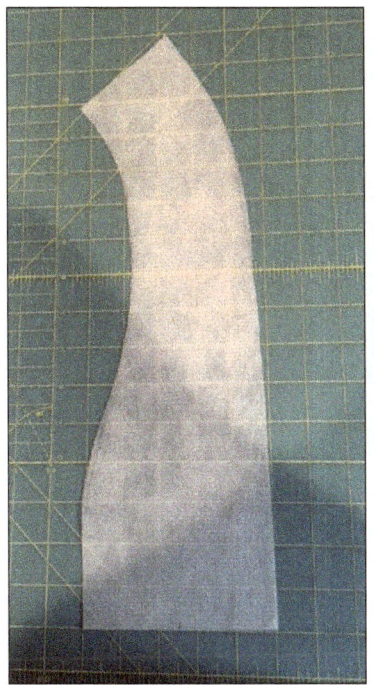

Cut out the pattern for the front of the contoured stole.

STOLEN MEMORIES

Sew both sides of the front together at the neck.

Now make the back of your stole (as above). In this case, you can fold the stole in half at the center back and pin your template to the fabric and then cut the contoured edges.

INSTRUCTIONS

 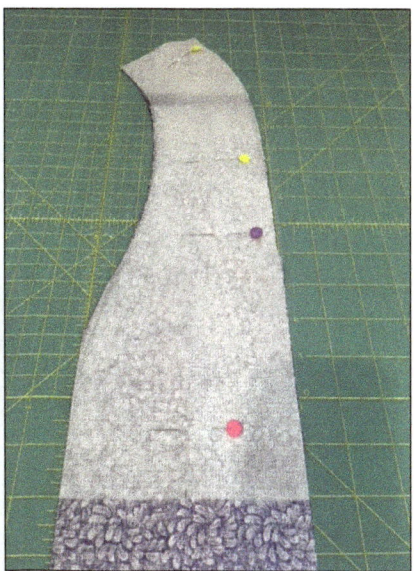

Sew both sides of the back together at the neck.

Starting at the center of the front and back sides, pin both sides together with the right sides of the fabric facing each other. As above, you are going to sew each of the two long sides from the center out, sewing one side all the way. I like to sew the inside curve first. On the outside part of the curve leave about 6–7" open (But this time, don't leave it open in the middle. It will be easier to work with the fabric to turn the stole right side out if the opening is not in the narrowest part of the stole.) so you can turn the stole right side out. Leave the lower edges (ends) open.

Sew inside curve first. Clip inner curves. Notch outside curves.

Sew outside curve and leave 6–7" open but not in the middle. Clip (inside) and notch (outside).

STOLEN MEMORIES

Turn the stole right side out and hand stitch the opening to close it. Then, as above, hem each end with the extra fabric from the back of the stole.

INSTRUCTIONS

You may recognize the finished stole as a gift for Pastor Paige Eaves.

D. HOW TO MAKE A STOLE STYLE TALLIT

Making a stole-style Jewish tallit is fairly easy, but it requires a bit of extra knowledge to do it properly. We read online that the "standard" length for a stole-style tallit for men is 76" but asked Rabbi Steve Glazer to take some measurements of a tallit that members of his congregation had made for him so we could create a pattern. Here's what he sent us:

> 1. Length—center of neck to bottom of each side = 35 1/2 inches; overall length = 72". (I'm 5'2"!).
>
> 2. Width at neck = 4"; width at bottom = 8".
>
> 3. Seems to taper briefly from 4" to 3 1/2" and then gradually widens to 8" at the bottom.

With this information, Don was able to create the following pattern:

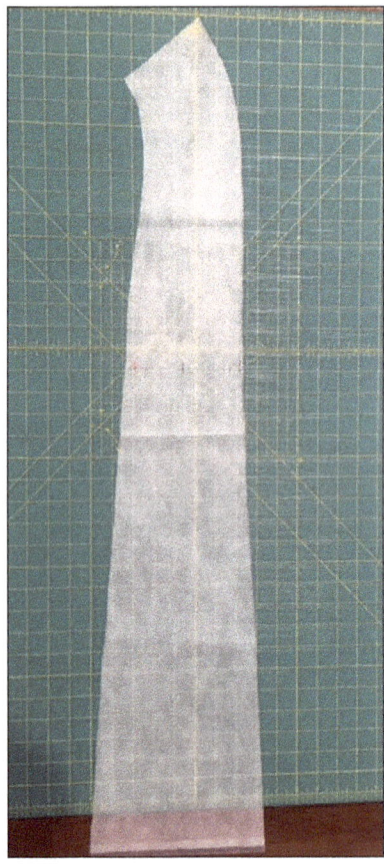

INSTRUCTIONS

With the exception of the hem (I simply closed the bottom seams vs. adding a hem before finishing the tallit by hand stitching the opening on one side.) and adding buttonholes at the bottom four corners for each of the rabbis to add their tzitzit fringe, the steps for making a tallit like the ones I made above are identical to that of making pastors' stoles. However, you'll need to cut the individual pieces of fabric for the front and the piece for the back wider to accommodate the gentle flare.

For the front of the tallit, all pieces are cut 8-1/2" wide and heights of either 2–1/2", 4", or 5" tall. Cut:

8 each 2–1/2"
8 each 4"
8 each 5"

Cut two lengths of the no-show mesh stabilizer 8-1/2" wide by 40" long.

Follow the same general instructions for making the back, remembering to make the lengths 8–1/2" wide to accommodate the flare.

7

Conclusion

I'd love to hear from you!

I hope you are as intrigued with these stoles and tallitot as I have become; that as you make them for others, you feel the blessings you hope to impart; and that those to whom you gift them will find them meaningful and use them to carry the banner for all impacted by dementia. My dream is to see many, many more clergy members wearing stoles and tallitot—in worship, at conferences, and when visiting local, state, and federal representatives as Alzheimer's advocates. If you'd like one for a clergy person who would wear and use it as we envision but are unable to make it yourself, please contact me. And, most importantly, please join us at ClergyAgainstAlzheimer's as we strive to make a difference.

When I'm not making stoles or tallitot (or hiking) I can be found advocating on FaceBook at Help Stamp OUT Alzheimer's or on Twitter @helpstampoutalz. Message me there or email me at ldeverman@icloud.com and send me a picture of your stole or tallit—preferably with your clergy person wearing it.

About the Authors

LYNDA EVERMAN HAS SPENT most of her adult life as a caregiver: for her mom who was paralyzed by a stroke, her dad with vascular dementia, and her husband with Alzheimer's Disease. These experiences inspired her advocacy for increased Alzheimer's funding for care and a cure.

She and fellow advocate Kathy Siggins conducted a multi-year national campaign for a semipostal (awareness and fundraising) stamp for Alzheimer's research. As a result of their efforts,

ABOUT THE AUTHORS

the first ever Alzheimer's Disease Research Semipostal Stamp was released by the U.S. Postal Service in November 2017.

Lynda is a founding member of three national networks under the umbrella of UsAgainstAlzheimer's and served as founder and convener of ClergyAgainstAlzheimer's. She is an editor and contributor to *Seasons of Caring: Meditations for Alzheimer's and Dementia Caregivers*. She and her husband, Dr. Don Wendorf, have served as editors for *The Leader's Guide for Seasons of Caring* and *Treasure for Alzheimer's*, both written by Dr. Richard Morgan; and were Senior Editors of *Dementia-friendly Worship: A Multifaith Handbook for Chaplains, Clergy and Faith Communities*. Lynda is on the Board of Beating Alzheimer's By Embracing Science (B.A.B.E.S.) (www.alzbabes.org) and has been recognized by Maria Shriver as a Woman of Influence in the Women's Alzheimer's Movement and included on her "Big Wall of Empowerment."

Lynda is a dedicated and outspoken advocate for those living with Alzheimer's and their care partners and, in September 2018, was honored with the inaugural UsAgainstAlzheimer's Advocate of the Year Award.

Don Wendorf, Psy.D. is a retired psychologist and marriage & family therapist, who practiced over 40 years, specializing in marriage therapy. He retired in 2013 to be the full-time caregiver for his increasingly stroke-disabled wife, Susan, after taking care of her while working for 15 years. She passed away in March 2014. He also helped take care of his mother-in-law (cancer), father (Parkinson's) and mother (Alzheimer's). Don currently serves on the Board of Cognitive Dynamics Foundation (www.cognitivedynamics.org).

Don has been a professional musician since his high school days, playing in a variety of jazz and bluegrass bands as well as writing songs. He combined all these interests and experiences in two books, one on marriage (*Love Lyrics: a Musical Marital Manual*) and one on the emotional struggles in caregiving (*Caregiver Carols: a Musical, Emotional Memoir*), both written primarily in song lyrics to be more accessible and memorable and to ease the pain a bit.

ABOUT THE AUTHORS

Don and his wife, Lynda, met when he contributed to her book, *Seasons of Caring: Meditations for Alzheimer's and Dementia Caregivers,* and together they have edited several additional books for caregivers. They are advocates for increased funding for research on Alzheimer's and related dementias and regularly speak to conferences, churches and advocacy groups on topics relating to dementia, brain health and caregiving.

In Memoriam

In loving memory of our family members whom we've lost to dementia:

    Alvin Joseph Ducote (1913-2001)

    Richard A. Everman, Sr. (1940-2012)

    Mary P. Wendorf (1921-2012)

    Susan Black Wendorf (1946-2014)

"The light shines in the darkness,
and the darkness has not overcome it."

—John 1:5 (NIV)

Bibliography

The Balm in Gilead, and Sanders-Brown Center on Aging at the University of Kentucky. *The Book of Alzheimer's For African American Congregations.* Midlothian, VA: The Balm in Gilead, 2017.

Berry, Kathy Fogg. *When Words Fail: Practical Ministry to People with Dementia and Their Caregivers* (DVD & Study Guide). Available from The Wesminister Canterbury Foundation at www.whenwordsfail.com.

Everman, Lynda, and Don Wendorf, et. al., eds. *Dementia-friendly Worship: A Multifaith Handbook for Chaplains, Clergy and Faith Communities.* London: Jessica Kingsley, 2019.

Huling Hummel, Cynthia. *Unmasking Alzheimer's: The Memories Behind the Masks.* Middletown, DE: lulu.com, 2017.

Morgan, Richard L. *Leader's Guide for Seasons of Caring: Meditations for Alzheimer's and Dementia Caregivers.* Columbia, SC: Create Space, 2015.

Morgan, Richard L., and Daniel C. Potts. *Treasure for Alzheimer's: Reflecting on experiences with the art of Lester E. Potts, Jr.* Columbia, SC: CreateSpace, 2015.

Potts, Daniel C., et. al., eds. *Seasons of Caring: Meditations for Alzheimer's and Dementia Caregivers.* Columbia, SC: CreateSpace, 2014.

Thibault, Jane Marie, and Richard L. Morgan. *No Act of Love Is Ever Wasted: The Spirituality of Caring for Persons with Dementia.* Nashville: Upper Room, 2009.

Wendorf, Don. *Caregiver Carols: a Musical, Emotional Memoir.* Columbia, SC: CreateSpace, 2014.

www.ingramcontent.com/pod-product-compliance
Lightning Source LLC
Chambersburg PA
CBHW072202160426
43197CB00012B/2487